JAN 1 9 2004

D1469385

I want to be A CLOWN

Ivan Bulloch & Diane James

STARRING

DENNIS

TOM

KIM

NICOLE

TWO-CAN
in association with
WATTS BOOKS

JOLIET PUBLIC LIBRARY

Photography © Fiona Pragoff
Illustrations Debi Ani
Design Assistant Peter Clayman

Copyright © Two-Can Publishing Ltd, 1995

This edition published in 1995 by
Two-Can Publishing Ltd, 346 Old Street, London EC1V 9NQ
in association with
Watts Books, 96 Leonard Street, London EC2A 4RH

Printed and bound by G. Canale and C.S.p.A, Italy

2 4 6 8 10 9 7 5 3 1

All rights reserved. No part of this publication may be reproduced, stored in a retrieval system
or transmitted in any form or by any means electronic, mechanical, photocopying, recording
or otherwise, without prior written permission of the copyright owner.

A catalogue record for this book is available from the British Library

ISBN 1-85434-326-2 (hardback)
ISBN 1-85434-291-6 (paperback)

CONTENTS

I WANT TO BE A CLOWN

There's a lot to learn but it will be well worth the effort! Being a clown is a great way to make friends! All the time you are learning new tricks, think about the great show you will be able to put on.

Find out how to use special face paints to create your clown face

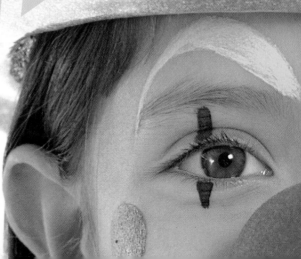

Design your own happy, or sad, face. This will become your new clown personality and you can use it over and over again

Keep an eye open at second-hand shops or jumble sales for old clothes that you can adapt – especially hats and shoes!

Try making your own clown hat from coloured cardboard

The bigger your shoes the funnier they will look. But remember to practise walking in them before the show

Before the show make sure you send out invitations and stick up posters in plenty of time!

Throughout this book you'll get lots of hints and tips to help you become a clown. The ideas here are just a few that you will discover. It's important that you think for yourself and develop your very own clown personality.

LET'S GO!

The first thing a clown needs is a face! You won't need a lot of expensive equipment to create this. But you will need a bit of practice and a mirror!

Use sponge-tipped sticks in the same way as brushes

Best brushes

It is worth investing in good quality brushes. You will need a couple of different sizes – thick and thin – and they should be soft so they don't hurt your skin. Always wash them when you have finished with them.

Don't rub your nose if you're using greasy face paints

Damp sponges can be used with water based face paints for covering large areas

Glitter gel adds extra sparkle. It looks good under the spot light!

Face paints

The simplest paints to use are water based. You can buy them in shops that sell party goods and places that deal with theatrical products. They will wash off easily with soap and water. Creamy face paints and greasy crayons are probably easier to find, but be careful because they can smudge. Use make-up remover to take them off.

Step one!

Plan ahead by sketching out your idea before you start painting your face. Then you will be able to work out which parts to paint first and which to leave till last! And you can sort out a colour scheme depending on what colours of face paint you have.

Most clown faces are really quite simple, with not too many different colours. Try exaggerating all the features, eyes, eyebrows, nose, cheeks and mouth. Turn over to the next page to find some tips for painting a happy face!

HAPPY FACE

Here is a simple face to get you started. Lay out your equipment before you get going and enjoy yourself!

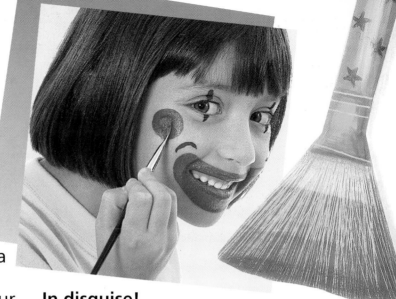

Get comfortable
If possible, sit in front of a mirror in a place where there is plenty of light. You'll find it easier if you can rest your painting elbow on a firm surface.

In disguise!
Next give yourself some big red cheeks. We used a small brush to make the black dimple marks either side of the mouth and the black lines above and below the eyes. To finish off your happy face, add some huge yellow eyebrows.

Nearly forgot! You'll need a big red nose. We bought this one but you could paint one on!

Smile please!
First paint on a big red mouth. We used greasy face paints. Remember that they smudge easily!

Happy now?
Now that you have finished your face, you have made the first step to becoming a proper clown. Later on in the book we'll help you put together a complete outfit – hair, hats, ties and ruffs. First, turn the page and try a sad face...

TIPS

★ If you are dressing up in full costume, put your outfit on *before* you start to paint your face!
★ Make sure your face is squeaky clean and dry before you start!
★ Put tops back on face paints when you have finished with them.
★ Tie your hair back to keep it well out of the way.

SAD FACE!

Happy clowns and sad clowns often perform together. Which would you rather be?

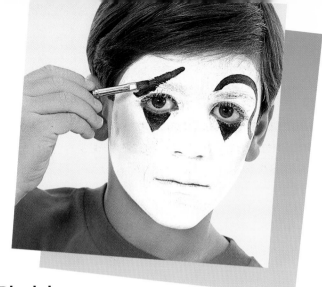

Ghostly white
Use a sponge and white water based face paint to cover your face. You may need to add a second and even third coat, but wait until each one drys before adding the next.

Black brows
Use a thin brush and a steady hand to add sad triangles under the eyes. Now paint on black eyebrows. Try making one straight and one wavy.

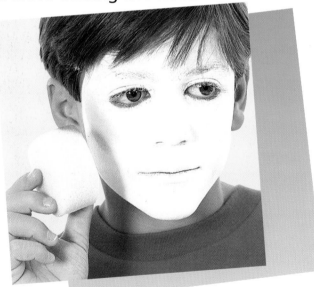

Pink glow
Before the final white layer drys, dip your sponge in a little red face paint and drag it gently along the line of your cheek.

Final touches
To complete your sad face, paint on some red lips and a blue teardrop.

A long tradition
White faced clowns are often called Pierrot – or Pedrolino – after a famous French clown who first appeared hundreds of years ago!

TIPS

★ If possible, it's best to use a different brush for each colour. This will save you jumping up and down to wash brushes.
★ As a rule, paint on light colours first.
★ Take your time. If you rush, it will show in the final result!

HAT PARADE

Here are just a few ideas for crazy clown hats to make and decorate for yourself.

Pierrot hat

Use a compass to draw a circle with a radius of about 20 centimetres on a piece of card. Or find a round shape that measures about 40 centimetres across and draw round it.

Have lots of fun decorating your hat. Try tinsel, streamers, pompons...

Cut a wedge shape out of the circle, like the one in the picture. Glue, or tape, the edges of the circle together to make a cone.

Fold the edges over until the cone fits your head.

Make a small hole either side of the hat and thread through a piece of elastic long enough to fit under your chin. Knot the ends of the elastic to stop them from slipping through.

Flowers for fun

First find an *old* straw hat. Now make some paper flowers. Cut two lengths of crepe paper, about 8 centimetres wide and roughly 30 centimetres long.

Snip a fringe along the lengths. Wind the strips round the top of a straw to make the centre of the flower. Cut a slightly wider and longer strip of a different colour. Wind it round the centre, pleating and crumpling it as you go. Tape the ends down.

Tape a wide band of crepe paper round the hat. Slot your flowers behind it.

Hairy hat!

Buy a glittery bowler hat from a party shop! Cut three lengths of paper to fit round the inside rim, leaving room for your face! Each strip should be slightly narrower than the next. Cut a fringe along the long edge of each. Glue the narrowest strip inside the rim. Do the same with the middle strip and the widest strip.

Don't forget to leave that gap so you can see out!

LOOKING THE PART

Your clown outfit won't be complete until you have a funny nose! And how about wearing a giant ruff, too.

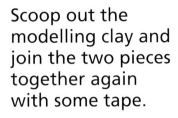

Scoop out the modelling clay and join the two pieces together again with some tape.

> Cover the join with more paste and paper and leave to dry

Spotty nose

Mould a piece of modelling clay into a nose shape. Tear up small strips of newspaper and make some paste.

Put a cup of flour into a small bowl and add water until it is like thick cream. Cover the nose shape with layers of newspaper and paste. About 3 layers should be fine.

> When the paste is dry cut through the nose with a craft knife.

Now paint your nose in bright colours. Ask a grown-up to make a hole either side at the bottom. Thread a piece of elastic through each hole. Make a knot in each end to stop the elastic from slipping through. Now try your nose on. What do you look like?

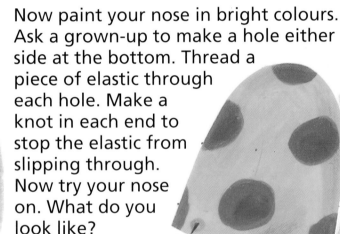

> Ask a grown-up to help you with this!

Fancy Frills

Now that you have made your nose, it's time to make a giant ruff to go round your neck! Cut two strips, about 25cm wide, from a pack of crepe paper. You can use the same colour, or two different colours. Make a row of small running stitches through both layers of paper along the long edge. Leave a length of cotton when you get to the end.

You may need some grown-up help for this!

Pull the long length of cotton gently to gather the stitches together. When the ruff fits neatly round your neck, fasten off the cotton with a couple of stitches.

You could make a multi-coloured ruff like this one!

TOPS AND BOTTOMS

Most clowns have their favourite costumes which they wear over and over again. You can make your own without spending too much time or money.

Over the top
Make yourself loads of badges to brighten up your outfit. Cut shapes from card and decorate them with paint or paper. Stick a safety pin to the back with strong tape!

Where to look
Clowns often wear loose baggy clothes so forget about how well your costume fits! Look for jackets and trousers at car boot sales, jumble sales and old clothes shops. Keep an eye out for old ties and belts, too.

Big and baggy

Look out for trousers that have lost their elastic! Thread a length of thin card through the slot where the elastic was to make a hoop. Keep your baggy trousers up with a pair of braces!

Glue or sew colourful patches on to cheer up a pair of boring trousers!

Bedroom slippers make good clown shoes

On your feet

The more ridiculous your feet look, the better! Clowns often wear shoes that are much too big for them, but you will need to practise walking in oversize shoes first Try adding stripey tights and spotty socks.

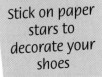

Stick on paper stars to decorate your shoes

SQUIRTY FLOWERS!

Now that you are dressed up and feeling like a real clown, it's time to prepare a good joke to play on a friend, or better still, another clown!

Smell my beautiful flowers!

Because this is is a wet and watery joke, it's best to make your flowers out of sponges and dishcloths!

A very special flower

Cut a circle from a piece of thin kitchen sponge and cut it in half. Next cut a length from a kitchen cloth for the inside of the flower. Cut a fringe along it. Fill a balloon with some water and push it into the end of a straw. Tie a piece of cotton round.

Wrap the fringe round the end of the straw and secure with a piece of cotton

Spray on a little perfume to make your pretend flowers smell good!

Now wrap the semicircle of sponge round the fringed cloth to make the outside of the flower. Tie a length of sewing cotton round to keep it in place. Your trick flower is now ready for action!

Make some more flowers in the same way but without the balloon and water. Gather the flowers together to make a bunch and wrap them up in a dishcloth. Remember which one is the trick flower so that you can squirt it when the time comes!

Why does this sort of thing always happen to me!

Invite a friend or another clown to have a sniff. Then squeeze the trick balloon!

You can use the trick flower over and over again but you'll have to fill it up between acts

BALLOON FUN

Making models from balloons looks complicated but it's really easy! You will soon be able to invent all sorts of different shapes to impress your audience and friends.

Special balloons

Modelling balloons are long and thin. You can find them in large toy shops. A balloon pump is a bonus if you are short of breath. Before you start inventing new shapes, there are a few simple techniques and tricks that you need to learn.

Twist it

Start by blowing up a balloon and knotting the end. Grasp the balloon between your fingers and thumbs and make a firm twist. You'll be amazed to find the balloon does not burst!

If you are making a model with a lot of twists, don't blow the balloon up completely.

TIPS

★ Practise making a particular balloon model over and over so that you can do it quickly without making any mistakes!
★ If your balloon bursts in the middle of the act, don't panic! Make a joke, blow up another one and then start again!

Sausage head!

You can make yourself a brilliant hat and get some practice at the same time. Start by blowing a long sausage shape. Knot the end. About 5cm from the knot make a twist. Hold the twist against your forehead and wrap the long length of the balloon round your head.

The long bit should fit around your head

Lock twist

When you are making a model you'll want to stop your twists from coming undone. At the point where you have made two twists, join them together and make another twist. This is called a lock twist.

Lock twist

Make a second twist where the long length meets the first twist. Now join the two twists together using a lock twist to keep your hat in position.

VANISHING CHAIR

Falling safely is a good trick to learn. You need to be a bit of an acrobat but you will get plenty of laughs every time you land with a bump!

Putting on an act
If you're the clown that is going to fall, try to act as casually as possible.

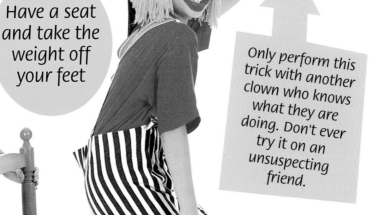

Have a seat and take the weight off your feet

Only perform this trick with another clown who knows what they are doing. Don't ever try it on an unsuspecting friend.

You know the chair is going to be whisked away but you must make the audience believe that you are being fooled! Whistle happily as you walk up to the chair and thank the other clown for the offer of a seat. Smile at the audience!

Make sure the chair is pulled well clear of the clown who is falling.

Uh, oh! This chair seems to be a lot lower than I thought!

TIPS

★ Practise on a mat or thick carpet until you are good at falling. A large cushion may help, too!
★ Use a small, light chair that is easy to pick up!
★ You could use the 'safety fall' for other acts, such as slipping on a banana skin.

Keep one knee bent and the other stretched out

Hey! What happened to that chair? It seems to have vanished into thin air!

Use your hands to help break your fall at the last minute.

Make a smooth landing!
When you sit down you usually bend both knees. But because you know there is no chair you need to land safely. The trick is to go down on one bent knee. Keep the other leg stretched out in front. Stretching your arms out wide will help keep your balance. Remember to relax when you hit the ground!

GREAT WATER CHASE

Working out routines is an important part of clowning. In this sequence it's the audience who are fooled, but at the end of the act everyone will be laughing together!

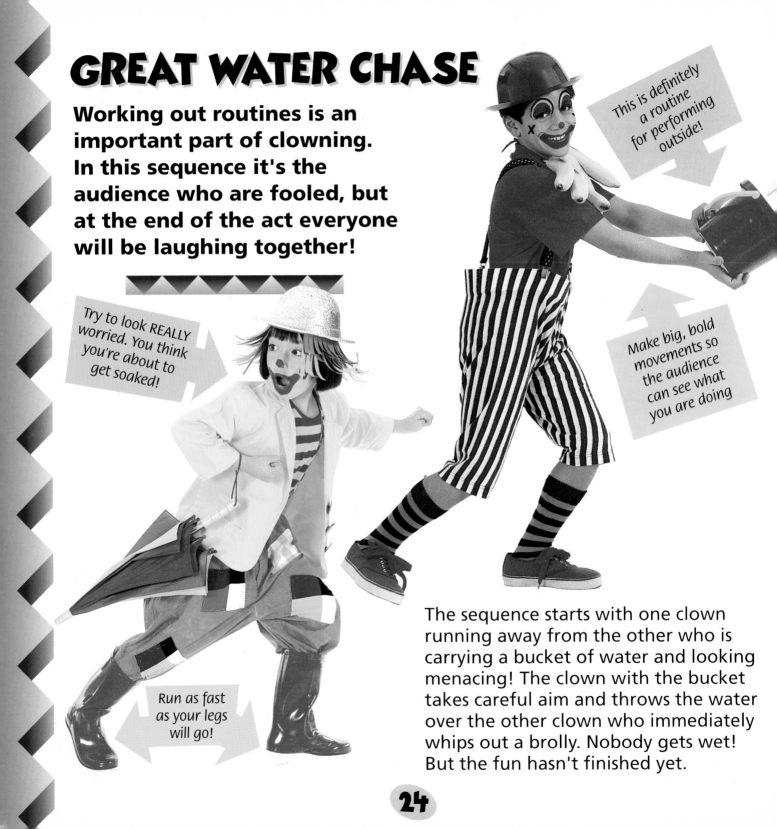

This is definitely a routine for performing outside!

Try to look REALLY worried. You think you're about to get soaked!

Make big, bold movements so the audience can see what you are doing

Run as fast as your legs will go!

The sequence starts with one clown running away from the other who is carrying a bucket of water and looking menacing! The clown with the bucket takes careful aim and throws the water over the other clown who immediately whips out a brolly. Nobody gets wet! But the fun hasn't finished yet.

It will be a few seconds before the audience realise they are not soaked with water! Instead they are showered with tiny pieces of paper! Both clowns can now turn to the audience – who are getting over the shock – and have a really good laugh. They knew what was about to happen all the time!

The expression on your face will help to fool the audience!

Good footwear for wet weather

Aim the bucket at the audience as well as the other clown

The tables are now turned. It's time for the other clown to get hold of a bucket and start the chase again! Taking careful aim at both the other clown AND the audience, she throws the contents of the bucket.

SUPER STRONG!

Make some 'trick' dumb-bells and pretend you have superhuman strength. Someone in the audience should know the trick, too!

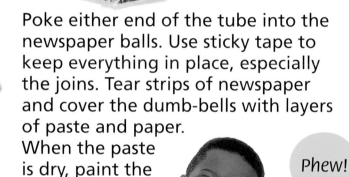

Poke either end of the tube into the newspaper balls. Use sticky tape to keep everything in place, especially the joins. Tear strips of newspaper and cover the dumb-bells with layers of paste and paper. When the paste is dry, paint the dumb-bells.

Phew!

The dumb-bells!
You'll need some newspaper, flour and water paste, sticky tape, and a long cardboard tube. Start with the weights. Scrunch some newspaper into two balls, keeping them in place with tape.

The trick
Tell your audience that you are
the strongest clown in the world.
Ask for volunteers to come and
show their strength by lifting your
dumb-bells. Make sure you choose
the person who knows the trick!
They will make a great act of trying
to lift the dumb-bells without success.
Send them back to the audience in
disgrace! Now take a deep breath,
bend down, and pick up the
dumb-bells with one hand. WOW!

GETTING READY!

It's nearly time for the big show and there's lots to do! Don't be afraid to ask for help and spend as much time as possible rehearsing.

Spreading the word

Once you have decided on a time and place for your show you can make the invitations and posters. Send the invites out at least a week before the show. Work out how many people you can fit into the space you have and don't invite too many people! You can always put on an extra performance!

Make sure you include all the details – time, date and place

Dress rehearsal

The day before your show run through the programme with full costume and face paint. This will give you a good idea of how long things take. Make sure you have enough helpers to move props, and possibly take part in acts where you need more than one person.

I definitely got the easy job to do!

Setting the scene

If you can, set up your props and stage the day before the show. This will give you more time to get yourself ready, and avoid any last minute panics. Keep a list of props so nothing is forgotten.

I'll be glad when the big day comes. This is hard work!

Glue small cardboard boxes together and paint them to make a circus ring

THE BIG DAY

After days and days of practising and making costumes and props the big day has arrived. It's time for the show. Now you can enjoy your day of fun and fame!

Ladies and gentlemen, please give a big hand to Tiny Tom, the funniest clown you'll ever see!

DON'T EVEN THINK ABOUT BEING NERVOUS! GET RID OF ANY TENSION BY HAVING A GOOD STRETCH AND SHAKE!

★

LEAVE PLENTY OF TIME FOR PUTTING ON YOUR FACE PAINT AND COSTUME

★

ASK SOME FRIENDS TO HELP YOU SET UP YOUR CIRCUS RING AND PROPS BEFORE THE AUDIENCE ARRIVES

It's useful to have a presenter, especially if there are lots of different acts

Clown costumes can be as weird and wonderful as you like!

Wait until the audience has settled down before you start your act. It's a good idea to begin your programme with something that will get them laughing as soon as possible! Once you've got the audience going everything will be easy! Try to vary the pace of your acts, so that you are not running around at top speed all the time! Perhaps you know a juggler or an acrobat who could join in and put on their own act.

Why don't you come a little closer and smell my beautiful flowers!

Hat made from one long, thin balloon

Put all the props in place before the show begins

Trick flowers made from sponges

Circus ring made from cardboard boxes painted in bright colours

INDEX

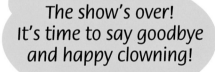

*The show's over!
It's time to say goodbye
and happy clowning!*